10 PAK - 1   *Candice James*

*"The lost dimension found.
This is what dreams may come."*

~ Candice James

Also by the author

A Potpourri of Paintings
The Still Small Voice of Soul
Spiritual Whispers
Atmospheres
Blue Silence
Call of the Crow
Imagination's Reverie
Short Shots 2
The Depth of the Dance
Behind the One-Way Mirror
The Path of Loneliness
Rithimus Aeternam
The Water Poems
Short Shots
City of Dreams
Merging Dimensions
The 13th Cusp
Colors of India
Purple Haze
A Silence of Echoes
Shorelines
Ekphrasticism
Midnight Embers
Bridges and Clouds
Inner Heart, a Journey
A Split in the Water

10 PAK - 1

THE LONG POEMS

by
Candice James

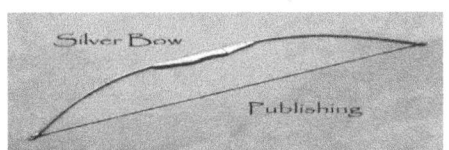

Box 5 – 720 – 6th Street,
New Westminster, BC
V3C 3C5   CANADA

Title: 10 PAK -1 The Long Poems
Author: Candice James
Copyright © 2025 Silver Bow Publishing
Cover Painting: "Top of the World"
painting by Candice James
Layout/Design: Candice James
ISBN: 9781774033432 (print)
ISBN: 9781774033449 (ebk)j

All rights reserved including the right to reproduce or translate this book or any portions thereof, in any form except for the use of short passages for review purposes, no part of this book may be reproduced, in part or in whole, or transmitted in any form or by any means, electronically or mechanically, including photocopying, recording, or any information or storage retrieval system without prior permission in writing from the publisher or a license from the Canadian Copyright Collective Agency (Access Copyright)
© Silver Bow Publishing 2025

Library and Archives Canada Cataloguing in Publication

Title: 10 PAK-1 : the long poems / by Candice James.
Other titles: Ten PAK-one
Names: James, Candice, 1948- author.
Identifiers: Canadiana (print) 20250123088 | Canadiana (ebook) 20250123622 | ISBN 9781774033432
  (softcover) | ISBN 9781774033449 (Kindle)
Subjects: LCGFT: Poetry.
Classification: LCC PS8569.A429 A612 2025 | DDC C811/.54—dc23

FOREWORD

The poems in this book are long poems set out in such a way as to allow the reader to rest on each page to fully digest the meaning and let their imagination run free to see the visuals and images the words are painting.

This layout gives the reader the best of experiences as they go through the poems and pages.

10 PAK – 1   *Candice James*

Ω Ω Ω

CONTENTS

A STARRY MOON DRIZZLED NIGHT / 9

DYING OF LOVE / 29

I WATCHED / 49

OH NIGHT! THE DESERT ENTOURAGE / 59

DREAMING, ABSENT, PRESENT, SURREAL / 71

THE EMPTY WOMEN / 83

PINK VELVET ROOM / 111

MEMPHIS ANDROMANYA / 129

EVEN NOW / 143

WOMEN AND CHILDREN / 149

10 PAK - 1   *Candice James*

Ω Ω Ω

A Starry, Moon-Drizzled Night

10 PAK – 1   *Candice James*

Ω Ω Ω

1

I walk the well traveled
pathways of my mind
under a starry, moon-drizzled night.
The keening of yesterday's voices
calls to me in soft bluesy melodies;
and the faces and bodies swaying
inside its charms are moaning
and calling me home.

2

The night is much too beautiful
to be real and yet, somehow,
I know it is more real
than the nights
I have been walking through
for eons and centuries
traveling through
the fog-riddled atmospheres
of my heavy-hearted
elusive dreams.

3

There is a cool pool
of pearl wisdom sparkling
at the edge of my vision,
at the edge of my hazy destiny.

4

I am struck stock still
in a sea of reckoning,
adrift in the wake of its waves,
gliding on familiar frequencies
and sweetheart whispers
that I once knew so well ...
long, long ago;
but now they have somehow
escaped my current being,
hovering just beyond
the shadow of the veil.

5

I am crossing over the threshold
    of life and death
into the land of never-ending spirit.
    There are no signposts,
        no guiding light.
There is not a single soul there
        to meet me.
I am alone and confused ...
        but not lonely.

6

I stand very still
inside this still stillness,
this arena of total quiet and serenity
wondering where all the people are.

7

I feel a brush of feather
or snippet of wind
catching at the nape of my neck
and circling my wrist
like a tender handcuff.

8

I am no longer walking
but I am moving.
I look down at the feet
I no longer have
and wonder, are they gone?
Or just covered in mist.

9

I hear a soft violin beckoning me
to fall deeper into the moonlit mist.
I espy a myriad of glittering eyes
watching me, piercing my soul;
and a million mouths are
moving in deafening silence,
speaking in tones
only they can hear.

10

I am drawn
into this strange domain,
as a fluid essence, through
a pulsating keyhole.

11

It's like I've been swimming
all my life in concrete
and now I'm finally drifting
with total ease
through a living ocean
of thoughtful dreams.

I am wondering if they are
really my dreams
or the dreams of all the others
I have known
somehow mixed into
the fabric of mine.

12

It's a glorious feeling
of all encompassing knowledge
wracked with terrifying visions
of the sins I've committed.

13

As I pass by
the people and voices,
each one touches my soul
for what seems like an eternity
rolled into a split second
of timeless time; and I am richer
for each emotion I am privy to
as the touch becomes
a birth and a tombstone
at the same time as
an hour becomes a minute,
then rolls into a second,
then disappears
down the rabbit hole
of recycled destinies.

14

I am quite amazed at the fact
that the faces I see
and the voices
that whisper and call my name
are unrecognizable to me.
Nobody I know or knew.

15

So, where am I?
What is this strange place?
Am I an enemy of great worth;
a prisoner to be put to death?
Or am I an entity
waiting to be crowned
with righteousness.

16

I do not see any buildings
or doorways.
No portals to escape into
and away from
this long and narrow road
of dangers, strangers,
blurred visions and
liquid horizons.

17

So, I climb
back out of
myself as I seem ...

that I can fall
back into
myself as I am ...

and continue to walk
on familiar ground,
as I weave in and out,
and move through
the well-worn,
yet overgrown, pathways
of my mind's many journeys.

18

As I come back into
myself as I am,
I see a starry,
moon-drizzled night
alive with the keening
of yesterday's voices,
at first a whisper,
slowly growing louder,
as they call to me
in coveted, familiar melodies.

Faces and bodies,
sway to the rhythm inside
their haunting whispers,
and lay in wait
asleep in my dream,
patiently biding their time
until it's time
for them to awaken
to call me home ...
once again.

Dying Of Love

10 PAK – 1   *Candice James*

Ω Ω Ω

1

A north wind howls
'cross a lone prairie
where ghosts whisper
to the hills at night.

Under skies peppered with
thousands of stars
lost angels fly with eagles
and doves.

2

In a place where clouds
were torn from the sun
and ice was shorn
from winter's last crop,
I awake in the cool
of dawn's light grasp
to dance with desire
in the jaws of death.

3

Tipping the scales
in a halfway house
at the edge of nowhere,
love lays mortally wounded
on a barbeque bed
of shattered moonbeams;
its heart sliced open,
and gutted like a Coho Salmon,
left charred and smoking
at the edge of death's door.

4

In the hollowed-out cry
of a cut glass scream,
with broken wrists
and scorched fingertips,
I try to place the hot sparks
of burning stars
back into my eyes
that I may see you again ...
even if only for
one moment more.

5

In the cracked aftermath
of the slow breaking dawn
I hide inside the catch
of my stale whiskey breath,
laced with single malt scotch
and finely aged death.

6

I drift and dream …
drift, drift and dream of you
and your stone-cold, chiseled heart
and iron clad teardrops
chained to my soul
with barbed wire songs
and cut-glass films.

7

In an empty concert hall
on a lone prairie
where thousands and thousands
of drunken fireflies
sing tributes to your angel face
and demon eyes,
I dip my pen in the fresh blood
of my heart
and write an epistle
to your cheating soul.

8

There's a bottle in my hand
filled with memories
that have been danced to death
by the blues;
then resurrected again
by a chorus of jazz
and the freshly ground spice
of worn-out tears.

9

And there's a room
where soft music keeps playing,
in a dusty dream
of slow burning embers.

10

At the darkened core
of a sweet reverie
there's a stone-cold sorrow
and hot melting snow
chained to the rust
of a dead memory.

11

Tonight we'll dance
in the devil's cabaret.
I'll take off my mask
and shed my disguise
and my wounded heart
will fall at your feet.

12

I'll barter my heart
to live in your love,
to ride high in the tidal rise
of your eyes.

13

I'll surrender my soul
in sweet crucifixion
to the melody fading
with your heartbeat.

14

Slowly ...

15

slowly I'm ebbing
into your soul.

16

Take my breath ...

17

take my breath away.

18

I've been dying of love for years.

I Watched

10 PAK – 1   *Candice James*

Ω Ω Ω

1

I watched the sky grow dark
      and strange
as the sun became draped in mist
and a charcoal cloud passed
through the needle
of its innermost eye.

2

I watched a wayward eagle circling
in random patterns above sky trails
too invisible for me to ascertain;
but I, like the eagle,
knew they were there
almost like strange radar
of the informational reciprocal
in the knowing soul.

3

I watched most of the night
before I fell into
a deep, disturbing sleep
rife with shadow people
and hounds chasing me until
I ascended to the charcoal cloud
and hid from them until dawn.

4

I watched the sun climb
over the horizon on supple knees
and well-worn elbows
finally lacing up its lunar shoes
and climbing the ladder
of luscious fast-fading stars
high, high, high up into the sky,

5

I watched the sun all day
until twilight closed in on its glow
and placed its purple scarf
around the neck of her essence
and eventually strangled her
with dark, honeyed fingers.

6

I watched the sky grow dark
and slowly dissolve
as the sun became
an expanding ink blot.

7

I watched until my eyes grew heavy
and the world disappeared
as my eyelids closed;
and sleep crept in
on soft supple slippers,

8

and I watched ...

no more..

O Nigh,
The Desert Entourage
(abridged version)

Ω Ω Ω

1

The entourage winds silently
through the whispering desert.
There is a heckling of Magpies
disturbing the peaceful firmament;
and a conspiracy of Ravens
staining a pale persimmon sky
high above the desert entourage.

2

I peer through God's discarded,
broken microscope
and see the stains left behind from
the tears of fallen angels.

3

I focus God's microscope and see
the Lord's Prayer written in gold
and an old, ragged scarecrow
climbing a mountain too high.

I see dead horses flailing and falling
into the callous arms of oblivion.
I see wreaths of blood red roses
floating in the darkness.

4

I walk on patches of neon grass
leaving luminous footprints
on the circular stepping stones
of seconds, minutes and hours.

I pry the time-worn, rusty hands
off the dusty clock of heaven.

It cracks the wheels of fate.
The world and the sky stop spinning
and I swear I'll never do that again...
never do that again.

5

I walk on driftwood, seashells,
agates, pebbles and feathers
scattered haphazardly along
the shorelines of life.

6

The waters of a looking glass fable
turn into a black onyx lake.

I drop a pebble from my heart
and a circle of drums appears
in the ever-increasing ripples
that glisten and sparkle
beneath a slow-moving sun.

7

I am a stranger in a strange land.
I see shamans dancing with dragons
and lions laying with lambs.

8

As the sunlit fingers of day
claw open the curtains of night,
I am still conversing with an adept
in the heart of this dream
I am dreaming I'm dreaming..

9

The sky shudders and darkens.
The magpies have fallen silent.
The ravens have landed.
The eye in the sky has closed
in the heart of this dream
it is dreaming.

10

"O Nigh" ...
the weary desert entourage
has quietly fallen asleep ...

fallen asleep

Dreaming, Absent, Present, Surreal
(abridged)

10 PAK – 1   *Candice James*

Ω Ω Ω

1

I am dreaming:

The moon is an angry angel,
that shows no mercy,
riding a silver stallion
armed with arrows and spears
stealthily stolen from winter's
hidden vault of destruction.

God smiles and winter
becomes spring,
becomes summer.

A beautiful cherub floats by
on a cloud of baby's breath.
Strands of golden hair
drift slowly past my eyes.
I reach to grasp one but cannot.

2

But still ...
      I am absent:

I am laying as an infant,
crawling like a baby,
walking as a toddler,
running like a child of the wind;
into the arms of adulthood.

3

I am present:

I lay in the lap of a lesser god,
inside the tree of life.
I watch the amethyst butterflies
glide, with eloquent ease,
through the glorious gardens
of paradise lost.

4

The wind picks-up; the sky darkens;
the atmosphere thickens.
The butterflies tremble,
change course and flee south
through a hurricane of nets,
wildflowers, and bees.

The sky spins faster and faster
until it becomes a flame.
I walk through a wall of
sweet smelling smoke
and climb into smooth mirrors
that dance in the mist
with the surreal shadows
of yesterday's children.

5

I become surreal:

I float down a river of pastel dreams
and torn nets.
I metamorphize and become
a human butterfly.
and the butterflies write their names
on my forehead
with the natural indelible dyes
of the earth.

I alter my universe
to fit with my thoughts then
slide through the kaleidoscope
veins in my eyes.

6

**I inhale
the invisible breath of the universe.**
A billion stars explode
in the noon day sun
and I fly through them all
with magnificent ease.

This day takes the shape
of a million months
and I'm finally at home at last
in my own private eternity.

7

**I exhale
the white diamond dust of death**
and suddenly the butterflies
turn on me unexpectedly
and erase their names
from my pulsating brow.

My wounded forehead bleeds
into torn antique cocoons
and the patiently waiting world
spins me slowly back Into
the heart of the dream.

8

I am dreaming:

The moon, the angry angel
the silver stallion and
the golden strands of hair
are dissolving in the acid tears
of the sorrowful sunbeams
raining down in broken streaks
from the petulant, jealous sky.

The essence of the dream
is fade-fading away.

Its taste on my tongue
is only a memory now
and I am floating and drifting
down from reality's cliffs
like soft newborn snow
in the shade of a summer breeze.

9

But still ...

   I am absent:

I am sleeping as an infant,
sobbing like a baby,
stumbling like a toddler,
swept-up like a child of the wind
into the eye of a hurricane
and into the arms of adulthood.

I am
dreaming, absent,
present, surreal.

I am
the absence of presence.

10 PAK – 1   *Candice James*

Ω Ω Ω

The Empty Women

10 PAK – 1   *Candice James*

Ω Ω Ω

*With all they love
stripped from them,
they are the empty women.*

Ω Ω Ω

1

Beneath a sky of a billion eyes
A dark demon smiles
and an angel sighs.

Inside a ship of iniquity
lost souls have no impunity;
and empty women
are shackled to pain
standing alone in a naked rain.

2

The empty women peer through
the ageless passing of years;
they stare though icicles
heavy with tears.

Carving prayers onto oblivion's face
they beg for redemption
and heaven's grace.
They peer through the edges
of timeless time
searching for a savior or a sign.

3

Submerged in the waters of eternity,
they wring their hands in futility.

Anxiously shaking and nervous,
they peer upward through
a slick muddy surface
and through the shafts
of murky sunlight.

They try to climb out of
their forsaken night.

4

These children of
a lost God's daughter
are innocent lambs
led to the slaughter.

With wounded hearts,
on bended knees
they claw at locked doors
that have no keys.

They burn 'neath a sea
boiling hotter and hotter.
Life's kinder to those
who walk on the water.

5

These empty women
stare hopelessly
into the fading night's
crass parody.

The are victims
of senseless violence
cowering in prisons
of self-imposed silence.

They are the living progeny
of pain, tears and death,
paying a price too high
with beleaguered breath.

6

They are too frightened to
watch their journey unravel
on the perilous path
they've been forced to travel.

They're unable to measure the
depth of their sorrow;
and they know there's no hope
for a better tomorrow.

7

They shiver with despair
and stare through the deep
at the rough path ahead,
and a mountain too steep.

Clad in old slippers
tattered and worn
they stand in the eye
of a scurrilous storm.

8

They walk as old ghosts,
from cold graves risen,
searching for exits
out of this prison.

9

With numb, bleeding feet
they walk, then they crawl,
trapped with no hope
of scaling Hell's wall.

They cry for old dreams
that were bartered or sold
and clutch to their breasts
all their secrets untold.

These empty women
keep paying the cost
For shell-shocked todays
and yesterdays lost.

10 PAK – 1   *Candice James*

*With all they love
stripped from them,
They are the empty women.*

10 PAK – 1   *Candice James*

Ω Ω Ω

10

A vigilante wind
is stalking their bones.
Late at night
it groans and it moans.

A hard rain falls
like a poisonous potion
creating a rough jigsaw
puzzled ocean
crashing a shoreline
of broken sea-shells,
harbouring secrets
it never expels.

11

Accentuating the absence
of a lost love
stars fall from the black velour
mantle above.

Embers burn out
in the ashtray of night,
caught in the jaws
of lust's fatal bite.

12

Crippled and trapped
in a nightmarish dream
these women are
the lost primal scream.

13

Spectres now,
erased by dawn's glove,
they're forgotten women
abandoned by love.
They're the elegy of
a dark broken moon;
a midnight eclipse
at the edge of high noon.

Their freedom and hope
were torn and tossed
into Hades pit
of blood, fire and frost
mixing them into
a hot pot of tears,
scalded hours
and charbroiled years.

14

Their footprints will disappear
leaving no mark:
No residue of
their cries in the dark.

No one will remember
their deep desperation.
This is their history:
the world's aberration.

15

At the edge of twilight's
purple eclipse
the stars sashay
and the moon dips.

The rain is streaking
old sunsets anew
in indigo shades
of a sinister blue.

16

When the rain started,
nobody knows,

But the feeling of hopelessness
grows and grows.

17

Empty women,
past the point of return,
these butterflies were born,
only to burn
twisting inside
the cocoon of death's kiss
in this moment that never was,
but always is.

18

Ghostly women,
hearts cracked at the mast,
still hanging onto
the invisible past.

Ravaged and trapped
in a nightmarish dream,
these women are
the primal scream.

10 PAK – 1   *Candice James*

Ω Ω Ω

10 PAK – 1   *Candice James*

*With all they love
stripped from them,
they are the empty women.*

10 PAK – 1   *Candice James*

Ω Ω Ω

PINK VELVET ROOM
(abridged and revised)

Ω Ω Ω

10 PAK – 1   *Candice James*

Yesterday memories
tumble lazily down
the swift moving rapids
of an ever-present atmosphere.

The rain drizzles and slides,
in a hazy opalescent mist,
whetting pages of long ago dreams
gently blurring my vision.

10 PAK – 1   *Candice James*

Up ahead at the crest of the hill
a pale beige house looms large.

The street seems half remembered,
and yet somewhat unfamiliar
until I reach the blacktop driveway
at 233 Second Street.
marked by a yellow broom tree
and a scarred white boulder.

A wave of relief flows through me
and I'm swept away to dreamland
on a colorful magic carpet.
Destination: a ceramic, pearl door
with a shiny, silver lock glistening,
basking lazily in the sanctity of
a sunbeam permeating the mist.

10 PAK – 1   *Candice James*

I stand anxiously at the door
wondering how I'll enter,
then out of the blue
an antique golden key,
etched with my initials,
manifests in my hand.

I open the door to one large room,
unsullied and untouched by time.

There is no past, present, or future.
There is only this moment;
this ever present, ever elusive,
                now.

I step inside, with great expectation,
and glide over a plush sea
of ivory coloured carpet
cresting and ebbing and coming full
beneath my mist-shrouded feet.

10 PAK – 1   *Candice James*

As I wade deeper into this sea
of cascading, endless memories
and ever-eternal moments,
all trepidation and fear vanish
in the warm wash and soft afterglow
of time forever suspended in time
in this timeless pink velvet room
alive with sunsets, moonbeams,
stardust and pulsating dreams.

10 PAK – 1   *Candice James*

My eyes hungrily drink in
the sparkling colors
and muted tones
as they slowly shift and drift
in the gentle roll of the room.

Glistening in vivid vibrance,
beneath the rainbow-streaked
antique crystal chandeliers,
two magnificent mahogany
grand pianos begin to play
in continuous harmony.

The beautiful intrinsic melding
of melodies immediately fills me
with the same indescribable awe
that painted my imagination
indelibly with exciting, vivid colors
and comforting gentle sounds
when I was a child.

10 PAK – 1   *Candice James*

I float toward the sounds
on my own private cushion of air
and run my hands gently over
the silky, pink, satin piano seats,
feeling the vibrations in the room
flow through my fingers,
beating perfect time
in unison with my heartbeats.

Haunting me, taunting me,
bringing me fully alive.

10 PAK – 1   *Candice James*

As I touch my fingertips
on the cool ivory and ebony keys ...
melody, piano and mind
become one, once again,
as it's always been
in this lost dimension of time
I've found inside my soul.

10 PAK – 1   *Candice James*

Over in the dimly lit corner,
a hazy movement catches my eye.
Something invisible and ethereal
is tugging at my sleeve.

I stand beside the imposing
exposition of a Pio Ricci painting,
almost holding hands with
"The Good Samaritan":
the six foot tall, detailed needlework
fire screen, regal and resplendent
in its French Rococo frame:

Suddenly, a change in the air.
The strong scent of Tabu perfume
permeates the still of the lucid
shifting, moody atmosphere:

The scent of a woman.
The scent of my mother.

The aroma and texture
of my childhood days
flood through my mind
and warm my soul.

And, for a while,
it's yesterday again.

10 PAK – 1   *Candice James*

Oh, the carefree days of youth,
so far and yet so near.
I swear I can almost taste
their liquid essence
sliding down my throat
like warm milk and honey
in the land of the lost.

From childhood's page
through middle age,
the smiles and tears,
the hopes and fears
wrapped in piano strings
and angel wings
breathe with a semi-life
of their own, reflecting mine.

10 PAK – 1   *Candice James*

The ceramic pearl door.
The pink velvet room.
Forever alive within me.

The lost dimension
found.

This is what dreams
may come!

10 PAK - 1   *Candice James*

Ω Ω Ω

10 PAK – 1   *Candice James*

Memphis Andromanya

10 PAK – 1   *Candice James*

Ω Ω Ω

1

I still see you in my dreams,
Memphis Andromanya,
standing deep inside my mind
at the broken crossroads
of yesterday and tomorrow.

I stand in a world of torn tears
unzipping the sky, carving my voice
onto the purple teeth of twilight
in the parallel flux of yesterday
and tomorrow.

Gray butterfingers of dusk
slowly spread dark honey
onto this moment in time.
There is a lonely face
watching a million miles
of melting dreams
slowly disappear into
a fading tear-stained horizon.

I still see you in my dreams.
Memphis Andromanya.

2

The zipper of time breaks.
Something in me breaks too.
I board eternity's train
to find you once again.

The past emerges
like a thirsty phantom
to drink from the pool of memories
I've untethered from time's marina
of lost days and long nights.

I see them strewn haphazardly
across the waters of Babylon
where we lay down to rest
in the arms of the angels;
but it's just a disappearing dream
like grains of sand in the crash
of a relentless incoming tide.

We walked through a harbour
of living wounds; the iniquitous
eye of midnight stared us down,
slayed the moon, sun and stars,
zipped us into its darkness.

10 PAK – 1   *Candice James*

When did we become one
with that darkness?
When did the lights go out
in your heart?
When did I stop noticing you
or your absences?
I am covered in caked on dust
from another century.
I'm trying to quietly creep
into your unsuspecting mind
but I feel like gritty sand
pushing into an empty shell.

I escape into a hazy dream:
steeplechases, fading ghosts,
broken water and abandoned
rowboats and canoes
come out to play with
my wandering nomad mind.

I'm almost where I want to be.
I'm surrendering to the draw
of my impending dreamscape
but my mind throws up
jagged images of you
to stop my journey
into unconsciousness.

You still haunt me
Memphis Andromanya.

In a darkened corner of my mind
I hear disembodied voices,
tangled in broken vines
and fractured veins of sound.

Above their hushed chanting
I hear your long-lost vows of love
echoing through drooping
derelict branches protruding
from my still beating heart.

Somewhere in my freefall
into oblivion's darkness,
a spark of sentience bursts forth,
jarring me into a state
of semi-consciousness
and, in this haze, I wonder
"Am I awake? Am I asleep?"
and then ... in sheer horror,
"Am I dead?"

I must be dead because
you are not here
and I always said
I couldn't live without you.

10 PAK – 1 *Candice James*

Was I lying? I take a deep breath
but don't seem to be breathing.
I panic! In a sudden sweat
the pounding of my heart
slaps me awake with a start.

Inside this cold, metal cocoon
I've wrapped myself in,
the drooling black lips of night
rasp and whisper my name
in a babble of muted incoherence.

A hooded dark angel
that knows no mercy
takes my hand and leads me away
from everything I've ever held dear.
He leads me away from
everything I've ever known
and whispers huskily in my ear
"I am the ghost
of Memphis Andromanya."
I fall into a deep-water sleep.

3

I awaken on the other side
of time and place and space.
Everything looks the same
but is insidiously different.
Windows are doors;
doors are windows,
and people are not real people
or they are real and I am not.

I see them but they do not see me.
I am an invisible, interloper;
unable to interact or make contact.
I am the damp ghostly residue
of the millions of dreams
these strangers in a strange world
are dreaming ... dreaming of me.

4

The dark side of night is fading,
burying slices of moonbeams
in its damp sticky pockets.

A reluctant sun pokes its eye
through fading beads of sweat
on the sky's forehead.

I am running away from
cardboard creatures and lost souls.
I'm tired of candling the night
down to the core of its wick;
tired of weaving phantom dreams
that cannot come true.

In the vapid eyes of a pale twilight,
breathing in foggy remnants
of second hand wishes and desires,
I churn them and burn them to ash
under the hot buttered sparks
from the wheels of my mind
grinding the tracks of my tears.

I hungrily drink in the horizon,
gulping it like a fine vintage wine.

10 PAK – 1   *Candice James*

On this hot thirsty night
of no reprisals,
the atmosphere hangs
in pockets of leather
chafing the edge of my requiem.

My face is wet, but I'm not crying.
The sky is crying, staining my skin.
I don't know when the rain started
but it shows no sign
of letting up soon.
Random drops cry out incoherently,
whipped by the want
of their own need,
relentlessly pursuing
the razor's edge of the one
running away in front of it.
The rain and I are trapped
in a rectangular, never-ending
circle game of tears.

I am a broken Cinderella
searching the streets of Nirvana
for my damaged Prince Charming.

5

The streets narrow;
the pavement flies away
and I fall through the ceiling
of an unmanned, runaway,
streetcar.
White time cracks
building to black.
Raindrops unstack.
Clouds come untacked
from the frayed fabric
of a weary, weakened sky.

I ride the rails of karma
seeking expiation from
this deep black chasm
as I squeeze the light
into lost works of art.

Winter's soul in speedy fashion
exits the mad masquerade ball
and throws off its tattered disguise.
I keep trying to climb
out of this unblessed hell hole
that keeps sucking me deeper
into it's fathomless depth.

10 PAK – 1   *Candice James*

A bony, accusatory finger
points to a blood-stained portrait.
It bears silent witness
to the depth of my fall.

I am pain, sorrow and death.
It's too much, but still not enough.

I am ripped from this universe
back into the torn tears
of my broken world and desolation
where I see your too familiar figure,
Memphis Andromanya,
standing there, long, strong and tall,
comfortable in your confidence,
resting on your shiny laurels;
but there is no rest for me.
No reprieve. No respite.

A wayward star glistens
on the whetted lips
of an outlaw breeze.
Across a pale, yellow sky
a rising moon sits astride
twilight's fading coat-tails,
riding silver sequined slices
of shadow and shimmer.

10 PAK – 1 *Candice James*

It spins haphazardly
and wildly out of control,
truly directionless with
no dedicated destination.

I, too, spin haphazardly
on a torn and tossed renegade wind,
dissolving in the misty tears
of a hot, pulsating, dying sun
under the half-mast eyelids
of a pale, yellow disintegrating sky;
the sky and I...
both of us old beyond our years.

The scarred black lips of night
tremble and whisper my name
in sandpaper tones
slowly growing louder.

The light of a rogue moon
illuminates a shadowy figure
slowly becoming clearer.

6

I see you approaching me,
Memphis Andromanya.

Unmasked and stripped
of all nuances and disguises,
we are ghostly apparitions,
caught in the cold clutch
of a damp ice-riddled hand,
trapped in the harsh hold
of a silent, strangled scream.

We are the lost souls
written in disappearing dialogues
on the dog-eared pages of eternity,
shuffling like worn out cards
into the wounded deck of night.

I still see you,
Memphis Andromanya,
standing deep inside my mind
at the broken crossroads
of yesterday and tomorrow...

where this day never ends.

10 PAK – 1   *Candice James*

Even Now

10 PAK – 1   *Candice James*

Ω Ω Ω

1

Saturday, early evening, December;
neon moon glinting buffed beams
polishing icy blue diamonds
to a fine glitter and shine
on the snow glazed street below.

We sat in creamy contentment on
the lush velvet sofa listening to
the soft satin voicings of Sinatra
and the echo of our heartbeats
as the snowflakes drifted and fell...
drifted, drifted and fell.

On that cold December night
in a summer state of mind
I looked into your eyes
and saw the promise
of another sunburnt July
dryng wanton teardrops
falling from the sky's eye.

2

Then came January evenings,
strong moons and ice glazed stars
dripping sequined teardrops
onto the broken dance floor
we circled so casually ...
oblivious to the sharp edges
and destruction that lay ahead.

3

Years later, alone on a sailboat,
drifting aimlessly
off the southern edge
of the Florida Keyes
I keep running the film
backward and forward,
forward and backward.
What I did and didn't do.
What you did and didn't say.
Not knowing then or even now
what you were thinking.

On the shelf in the cabin
there's a photo of us standing
glinting beneath a neon moon
and on the table, a stack of love
letters I wrote ...
but never did send to you.

Earlier today I wrote
another love letter to you
pouring my heart out,
crying my eyes out,
kissing the tear stained pages
knowing I'd never send them to you.

4

I reach for my guitar
and once again I become
the gypsy singer
you fell in love with long, long ago
on a cold December night.

I imagine you, tonight,
High up on a mountain
On the other side of the world
Where the snow is softly falling
And I wonder...
if you're remembering too

I want to tell you everything
but even now,
after all this time,

I can't.

10 PAK – 1   *Candice James*

Women and Children

10 PAK – 1   *Candice James*

Ω Ω Ω

10 PAK – 1   *Candice James*

Angels, magically performing
miracles in spiralling circles of hope
atop the ceremonial seas of destiny,
prevail upon the tides of time.

A multi-coloured rainbow
pulsates against a mist covered sky.
Twilight and sleep
conjure-up dreams
of a golden hued city flanked by
ancient warriors standing guard.

Gleaming in eternity's mirror,
white robed sages and shamans
encased in golden auras
elusively flow and ebb
through a twinkle of stars
and the scriptures of heaven.

Returning and changing shapes,
this ultra-feminine caucus
rises like a laureate spell
enshrouded in a glorious cause.

Women and children
pray to the angels:

*"Leave these men alone.
Do not trifle with their souls."*

Pentecostal aftermaths rain down,
from the beads of sweat
falling from heaven's brow,
and dedicate themselves
to the total annihilation
of hellish atrocities
and hidden blasphemies.

Ghosts and aging philosophers,
declining pride and insolence,
have been blessed and tasted
the eternal flame of knowledge.

Unable to grasp the true gifts of love
offered by their women,
they shall never surrender
their crowns of indifference
and swords of thorns
to speculation, risk or chance.

Familiar with meat and drink,
flesh and blood,
they enlist their saviours and angels
to battle the deadly sins.

Women and children
pray to the angels:

*"Leave these men alone.
Do not trifle with their souls"*

Vengeance serves its own needs
parading through disguises
that none may truly know her.
Passion put asunder
claws at the steamy window pane:
A cat scratching for sustenance
eking out a frantic desperation.
Shrieking talons
against a glass shorn world.

Eyes that have witnessed
too many luke-warm altars
search for gods in vain
be they heavenly or earthbound.

10 PAK – 1   *Candice James*

Blood congeals
on the written word
that dissolves in acid teardrops
as the women and children weep
for the forgotten rainbows
and disappearing skies.

Midnights come and midnights go
stabbing the marauding days
with sharp ebony stilettoes.
Seams of a dark navy skirt
shred then split wide open
over a shot silk evanescent slip,
dawn and dew dissolving
only an embrace away.

10 PAK - 1   *Candice James*

Deeds and gifts
are not one in the same.
Connected as they appear to be
they have separate luminosities,
separate densities,
an obscure separation of identities.

Fresh water streams
gorge their niche
through scarred mountain trails
still alive with the bated breath
of the ancients
adrift and ablaze
in their own eternities.

These things are spoken of softly
and whispered through death's
chilled and chapped lips.

Women and children
pray to the angels:

*"Leave these men alone.
Do not trifle with their souls."*

Promises made but never heard.
Questions locked in the ears of hell.
Satyrs galloping carelessly through
a herd of star blessed unicorns.
Thorns in a lion's paw.

Luck and the devil reign supreme
over the land of the lost,
the forlorn and forgotten.

10 PAK – 1   *Candice James*

Seas churn with strife
destroying the fabric of life.
Spirits and entities
lacerate their wrists
spilling crimson life
to sear each other's wounds,
trying on each other's soul
uncomfortable with the sizes
that don't quite fit.

Pain and torture, real as they seem,
Chafed with coals
and raw with diamonds
are only feelings of the flesh.

Kingdoms have crumbled.
Seasons have stumbled
under the tears
of these women and children,
inside the prayers
of these mothers and virgins;
and still these men
do not deign to understand
the source, the reason
for their sanctuary.

Women and children
still pray to the angels.

*"Leave these men alone.
Do not trifle with their souls."*

Angels magically performing
miracles in spiralling circles of hope
atop the ceremonial seas of destiny
in another time and space
elude, evade, and stay hidden from
these pious women and children.

Prayers vanish into lost horizons,
fading surreal ink blots
in a fog encrusted valley.
Illusions manifest
in smooth satin sheaths.
Gleaming sabres in a shot silk sky
peering through the eye of midnight.
People and shadows pass
through the callous hands
that sift the sands of time.
Their presence, never registered,
they float as spirits on high
delving and diving through the eyes
of a thousand living needles.

10 PAK – 1   *Candice James*

Hands and hearts
riddled with bloodstains,
embedded, indelibly etched
in the fabric of their souls,
these men have given their best,
tasted the fruits of victory
and worn the wounds of defeat.

Commanding hope.
Seeking asylum.

Women and children speak
through the souls of these men.

***"Leave their words alone.
Do not trifle with their thoughts."***

10 PAK – 1   *Candice James*

Ω Ω Ω

Women and children,
Angels and prayers,
The keepers of the keys:

To the stars.
To eternity.

Candice James is a writer, poet, visual artist, musician, singer/songwriter, and book reviewer. She completed her 2nd three-year term as Poet Laureate of The City of New Westminster, BC CANADA in June 2016 and was appointed Poet Laureate Emerita in November 2016.

She is Founder of: Royal City Literary Arts Society; Past President Federation of British Columbia Writers. Candice is a full member of the League of Canadian Poets, She has received Pandora's Collective Vancouver Citizenship Award; and the Bernie Legge Artist/Cultural award.

Her poetry has appeared in many international anthologies and her poems have been translated into Arabic, Italian, Bengali, Farsi and Chinese. Her artwork has appeared in Duende Magazine and in the "Spotlight" at Goddard College of Fine Arts, Vermont, USA and her poetry inside and artwork ("Unmasked") on the cover of Survision Magazine, Dublin, Ireland and her poetry and artwork have appeared in Wax Poetry Art Magazine Canada.

FOR MORE INFORMATION VISIT
website www.candicejames.com

www.ingramcontent.com/pod-product-compliance
Lightning Source LLC
Chambersburg PA
CBHW052142070526
44585CB00017B/1940